Sally Ride
The Sky's the Limit

Paolo Bindi

I0808889

Infomax Readers

Rosen Classroom™

New York

Published in 2014 by The Rosen Publishing Group, Inc.
29 East 21st Street, New York, NY 10010

Book Design: Katelyn Londino

Photo Credits: Cover (Sally Ride) en.wikipedia.org/wiki/File:Ride-s.jpg/Wikipedia.org; cover (space shuttle) en.wikipedia.org/wiki/File:Space_Shuttle_Challenger_(04-04-1983).JPEG/Wikipedia.org; p. 5 Express Newspapers/Archive Photos/Getty Images; p. 7 Brian Russell/Associated Press; pp. 9, 11 Space Frontiers/Archive Photos/Getty Images; p. 13 SCIENCE SOURCE/Photo Researchers/Getty Images; p. 15 BAVARIA./Lifesize/Getty Images; p. 17 Sandy Huffaker/Getty Images News/Getty Images; p. 19 Dominic Hart/NASA.gov; p. 21 Justin Sullivan/Getty Images News/Getty Images; p. 22 en.wikipedia.org/wiki/File:Top_of_Atmosphere.jpg/Wikipedia.org.

ISBN: 978-1-4777-2451-4
6-pack ISBN: 978-1-4777-2452-1

Manufactured in the United States of America

CPSIA Compliance Information: Batch #CS13RC: For further information contact Rosen Publishing, New York, New York at 1-800-237-9932.

Contents

Early Life

Sally Ride was the first American woman to go into outer space. Through her success, she showed people that there's no **limit** to what women can do!

Sally was born on May 26, 1951. She grew up in Los Angeles, California, with her parents and her sister. From a young age, Sally showed a great interest in sports and learning about new things.

Sally loved to read and play tennis. She was one of the best young tennis players in the country!

When she was in high school, Sally became interested in physics. This kind of science studies all matter that exists in Earth and space. A great teacher, Elizabeth Mommaerts, taught her how cool science can be.

After high school, Sally thought she might become a famous tennis player. However, she went to a **college** so she could learn more about English and physics.

Studying physics helped Sally understand space travel.

Shuttle

Joining NASA

Sally was very smart and worked hard. One day, she heard that NASA was hiring astronauts for space flights. Astronauts are people who travel in outer space. Sally applied for the job, along with about 8,000 other people.

Because she was so smart, NASA picked her! She had to go through a lot of training before she could be a real astronaut.

It was 1977 when Sally found out NASA needed astronauts. This was the first time women were allowed to apply.

JOHN FABIAN
N. THAGARD
SALLY K. RIDE
CRIP

Training to be an astronaut takes a lot of hard work. Sally learned about weather, computers, math, and science. She also had to learn how to fly! She loved flying so much that she even did it for fun.

Not everyone who trains gets to go into outer space. However, NASA chose Sally to go on a space flight because she was good at fixing problems and she worked well on a team.

Playing sports made Sally a good team player. It's important for astronauts to work as a team!

Up, Up, and Away!

On her space flight, Sally was a mission **specialist**. A mission is a task that's given to a person or a group of people. Each space flight had a mission to help NASA learn more about space and Earth while they were away.

Sally's mission began on June 18, 1983. She and four other crew members flew to space on the *Challenger*, a **space shuttle**.

On June 18, 1983, Sally became part of history as the first American woman to go into outer space.

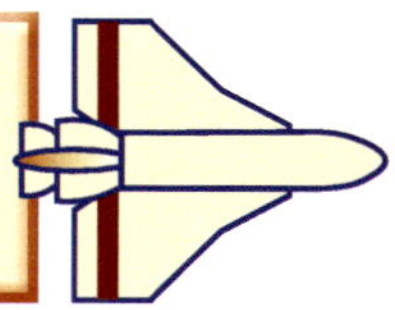

CHALLENGER
McDONNELL DOUGLAS

Sally's first mission was a success! At only 32 years old, she was the youngest person ever to go into outer space. After the flight, she told people that she had a lot of fun in space.

In 1984, she flew to space for a second mission. She was supposed to go on another flight after this, but the *Challenger* had a bad accident.

In January 1986, the *Challenger* exploded soon after it took off, killing the whole crew. Americans were very sad about the accident.

USA
NASA
Challenger

Special Jobs

Sally **investigated** the *Challenger* accident. She and other specialists found out what went wrong. After this, Sally never went to space again, but she had other jobs at NASA. She wrote a special report that told people how important it was for America to lead more space missions.

Sally left NASA in 1987 and became a professor. She taught physics and also directed the California Space Institute.

Sally Ride knew a great deal about science and space, so she spoke and wrote about these subjects often.

Sally remembered how her teacher, Elizabeth Mommaerts, had started her love for science. Sally made it her mission to teach kids all about science. She started programs that made learning about science easy and fun. That way, more kids would follow their dreams to be scientists.

Sally also wrote seven children's books about science, including *To Space and Back* and *Mission: Planet Earth*.

Sally thought everyone should have a chance to learn about science.

Sally Ride Science Club Festival

Honoring a Hero

Sally Ride spent many years trying to make science and math **education** better. She founded a company called Sally Ride Science and worked there for the rest of her life. Sally died on July 23, 2012, at only 61 years old.

Sally was honored by many people for the work she did. We remember her today as an example of a woman's ability to accomplish anything.

Sally Ride was honored with a place in the California Hall of Fame in 2006.

HALL OF
AT THE

Sally Ride's Life

2012
Sally dies.

2006
Sally joins the California Hall of Fame.

2001
Sally founds her company, Sally Ride Science.

1989
Sally becomes a professor of physics in San Diego.

1988
Sally joins the National Women's Hall of Fame.

1983
Sally goes on her first space flight.

1978-1982
Sally trains to be an astronaut.

1977
Sally applies to be an astronaut.

1951
Sally is born.

Glossary

college (KAH-lihj) A school where people go to learn after they finish high school.

education (eh-juh-KAY-shun) The act of learning or training.

investigate (ihn-VEHS-tuh-gayt) To look into something closely and carefully to learn the facts.

limit (LIH-muht) The point at which something ends.

space shuttle (SPAYS SHUH-tuhl) A spacecraft used to carry people and supplies back and forth between Earth and space.

specialist (SPEH-shuh-lihst) A person who knows a lot about something.

Index